Now We Are Sick
An Anthology of Nasty Verse

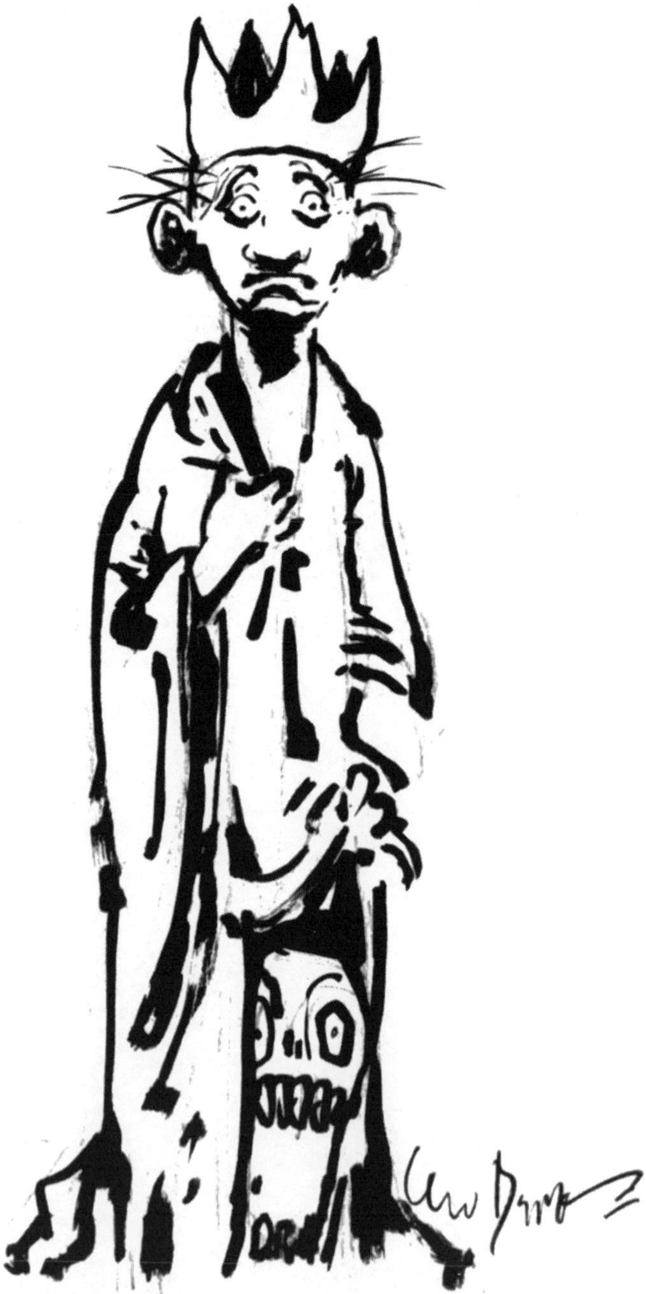

Now We Are Sick
An Anthology of Nasty Verse

Edited by
Neil Gaiman and Stephen Jones

Illustrations by
Andrew Smith and Clive Barker

Cover Art by
Gahan Wilson

DreamHaven Books
Minneapolis, Minnesota ✦ 2005

Now We Are Sick

NOW WE ARE SICK Copyright © Neil Gaiman and Stephen Jones 1991, 1994, 2005.

Acknowledgements

"Now We Are Sick" Copyright © Neil Gaiman and Stephen Jones 1986.
"A Slice of Life" Copyright © Diana Wynne Jones 1986.
"Auntie Ethel" Copyright © Richard Hill 1991.
"You Always Eat the One You Love" Copyright © Kim Newman 1991.
"Chocolate and Worms" Copyright © David S. Garnett 1991.
"The Dangers of Color TV" Copyright © Simon Ian Childer 1991.
"The Children's Hour" Copyright © Alan Moore 1986
"Radio Nasty" Copyright © Stephen Gallagher 1991.
"Something Came Out of the Toilet" Copyright © Harry Adam Knight 1991.
"The Secret Book of the Dead" Copyright © Terry Pratchett 1991.
"Mummy's Blocked the Lav Again" Copyright © John Grant 1991.
"Rice Pudding" Copyright © Brian Aldiss 1991.
"Aboard the Good Ship 'Revenger'" Copyright © Galad Elflandsson 1991.
"The Dream of Omar K. Yam" Copyright © David Sutton 1991.
"You're Deceased, Father William" Copyright © Colin Greenland 1991.
"A Landlady's Lament" Copyright © Ramsey Campbell 1986.
"The Borgia Brats" Copyright © Garry Kilworth 1991.
"Another Cursed House Story" Copyright © John M. Ford 1986.
"Waiting . . ." Copyright © James Herbert 1991.
"The Thing at the Top of the Stairs" Copyright © Sharon Baker 1991.
"Things that Go Bump in the Night" Copyright © Ian Pemble 1991.
"In the Dark" Copyright © Storm Constantine 1991.
"Lights Out" Copyright © Alex Stewart 1991.
"A Mother's Tender Love" Copyright © Jo Fletcher 1986.
"Catcawls" Copyright © Samantha Lee 1991.
"The Haunted Henhouse" Copyright © Jessica Amanda Salmonson 1991.
"When the Music Breaks" Copyright © R.A. Lafferty 1991.
"Nasty Snow" Copyright © Jody Scott 1991.
"Why Private War" Copyright © Gene Wolfe 1986.
"The Answering Machine" Copyright © Somtow Sucharitkul 1991.
"Warning: Death May be Injurious to Your Health" Copyright © Robert Bloch 1991.
"About the Contributors" & "About the Artists" Copyright © Stephen Jones and Neil Gaiman 2005.

Interior Illustrations Copyright © Andrew Smith 1991, 2005.
Cover Illustration Copyright © Gahan Wilson 1994.
Frontis Illustration Copyright © Clive Barker 1991.
Hand Illustration Copyright © Robert T. Garcia 2005.
Design by Robert T. Garcia, Garcia Publishing Services // www.gpsdesign.net

DreamHaven Books
912 W. Lake St.
Minneapolis, MN 55408
www.dreamhavenbooks.com

ISBN 1-892058-10-3
PRINTED IN THE UNITED STATES OF AMERICA

CONTENTS

Introduction

Now We Are Sick   The Editors   11

Nasty Habits

A Slice of Life   Diana Wynne Jones   15
Auntie Ethel   Richard Hill   17
You Always Eat the One You Love   Kim Newman   18
Chocolate and Worms   David Garnett   19
The Dangers of Color TV   Simon Ian Childer   22
The Children's Hour   Alan Moore   23
Radio Nasty   Stephen Gallagher   25
Something Came Out of the Toilet   Harry Adam Knight   27
The Secret Book of the Dead   Terry Pratchett   31
Mummy's Blocked the Lav Again   John Grant   33

In Loving Memory

Rice Pudding   Brian Aldiss   37
Aboard the Good Ship "Revenger"   Galad Elflandsson   39
The Dream of Omar K. Yam   David Sutton   42
You're Deceased, Father William   Colin Greenland   44

Less Welcome Tenants

A Landlady's Lament   Ramsey Campbell   49
The Borgia Brats   Garry Kilworth   53
Another Cursed House Story   John M. Ford   55
Waiting . . .   James Herbert   58
The Thing at the Top of the Stairs   Sharon Baker   60
Things That Go Bump in the Night   Ian Pemble   62

Night Fears

In the Dark	Storm Constantine	69
Lights Out	Alex Stewart	71
A Mother's Tender Love	Jo Fletcher	73
Catcawls	Samantha Lee	75
The Haunted Henhouse	Jessica Amanda Salmonson	79
When the Music Breaks	R.A. Lafferty	80

Adults Only

Nasty Snow	Jody Scott	85
Why Private War	Gene Wolfe	87
The Answering Machine	S.P. Somtow	89

Epilogue

Warning: Death May Be Injurious to Your Health	Robert Bloch	97

This book is
Clive Barker's fault
— blame him.

Introduction

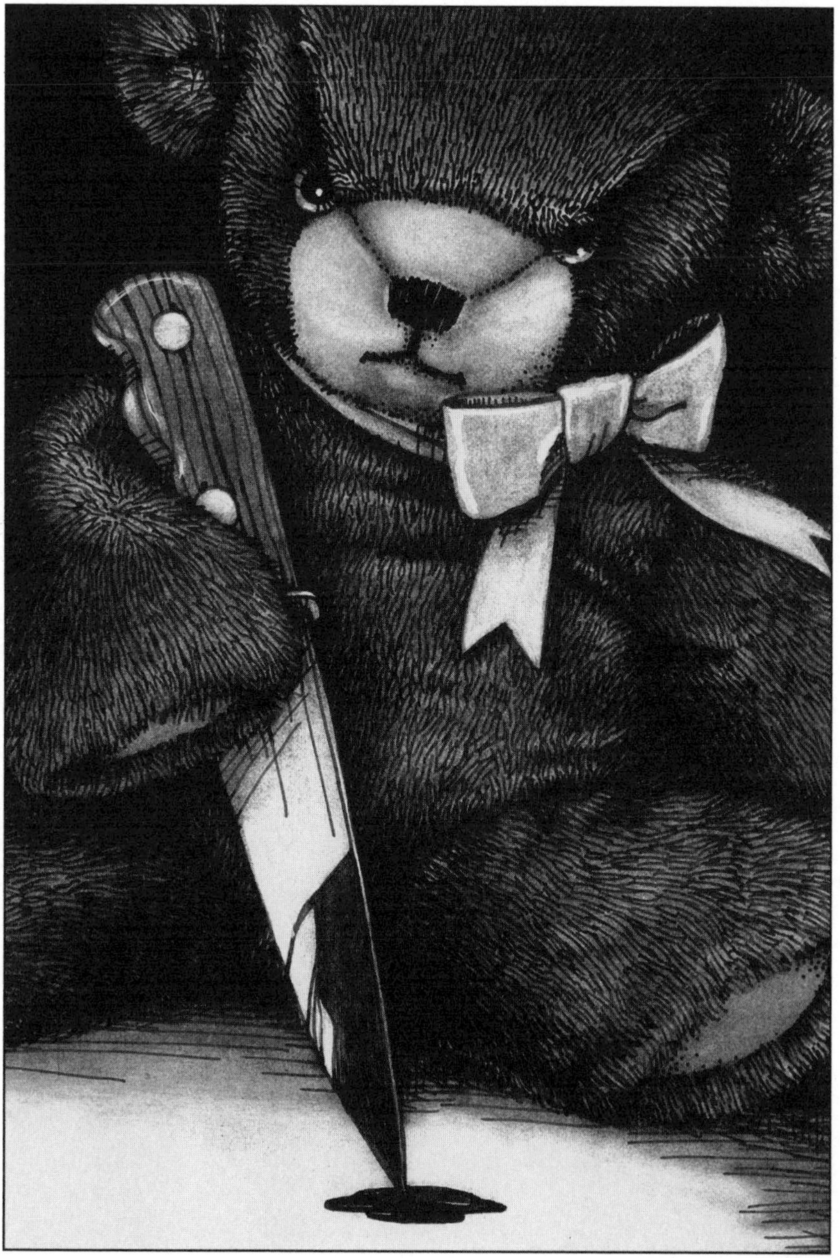

NOW WE ARE SICK
The Editors

Dear Child, may our tales hereafter
Give you cause for happy laughter;
Let them tint your cheeks with joy
(Pink for girl, and blue for boy),
May they never make you quail
Shiver, quiver, or turn pale . . .

If our fancies, grues and gories,
Ever cause you needless worries
We are very *very* sorry —
But they're only fairy stories.

Dreams won't eat you, nor will mist,
Wicked witches don't exist,
Clowns are friendly, rabbits tame,
Dead don't walk nor mutants maim . . .

This, and more, we here declaim,
(Just be careful, all the same).

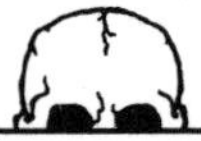

Nasty Habits

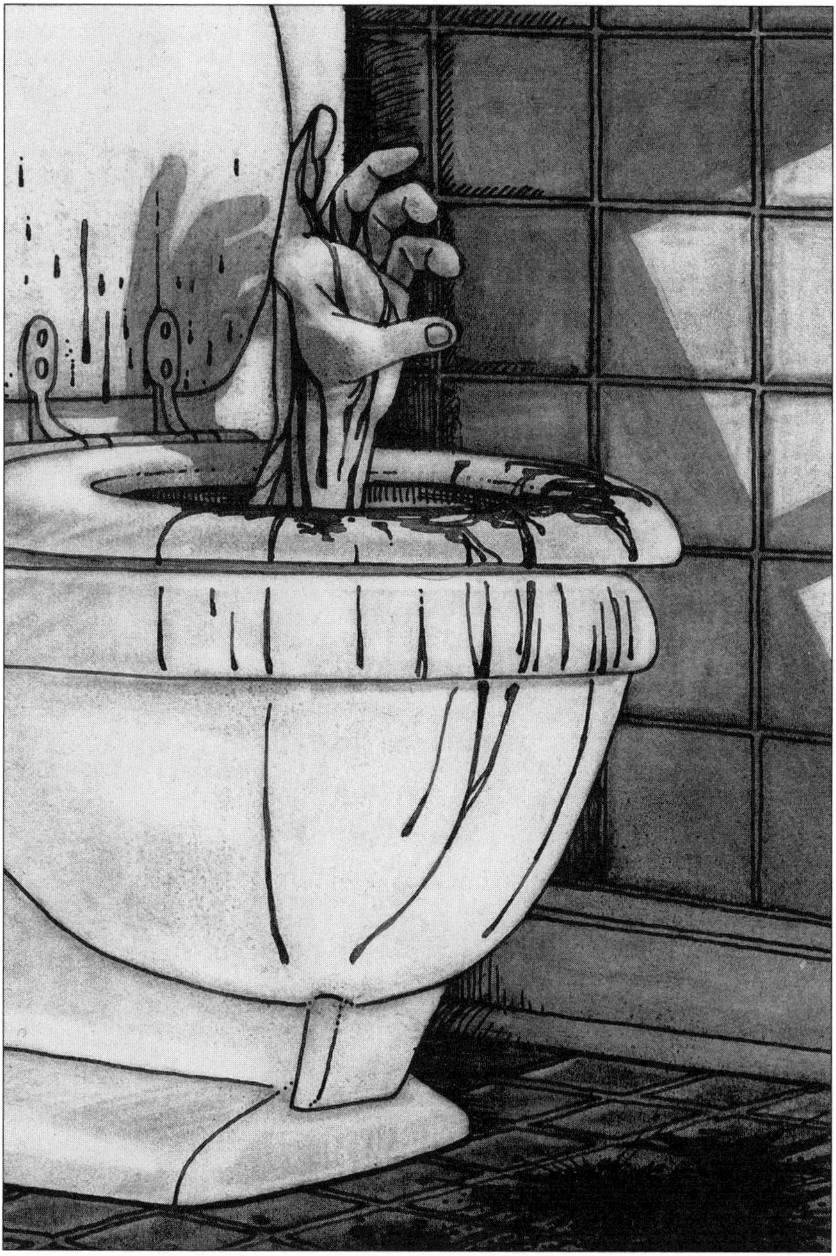

A SLICE OF LIFE

Diana Wynne Jones

Monday: What's become of Mr. Grundy?
He hasn't been in school all Monday
A rumor went round in Assembly:
"Our Headmaster's gone to Wembley
To have a rest, and Mrs. Todd
Will be in future known as God."
I found some toenails in my stew.
I don't believe that rumor's true.

Tuesday: Mr. Grundy's hair is wavy
Like the hair in Tuesday's gravy,
And guts *do* look like macaroni.
I know the sausages were phony —
Mine had three joints of bone inside
And could have been a finger, fried.
It wouldn't chew, I had to suck it.
I think Grundy's kicked the bucket.

Wednesday: Mrs. Todd has bumped off Grundy:
We think she did it first thing Monday,
We're sure these baked beans really *are* toes,
So no one touched the tinned tomatoes
Or opened up their ravioli

Or dared to eat jam roly-poly.
We all made do with mushy peas,
Which *could* be Grundy's brains in cheese.

Thursday: Most people brought packed lunch to school,
But my Mum says I'm a fool
And won't believe a word I say!
They served up Grundy's legs today
In round, thin slices from the freezer,
Just the size to fit a pizza.
I hope Mum sees me on the telly —
I've found his eyeball in my jelly.

Friday: Mr. Grundy's back! He's here!
No teethmarks on him anywhere!
And Mrs. Todd sits looking sweet —
But we know what we've had to eat,
And everybody wants to know
Whose eyeball is this? Whose big toe?
And if those sausages weren't Grundy,
Who *have* we had for lunch since Monday?

AUNTIE ETHEL
Richard Hill

There were policemen and men from the papers
And a nice man from the BBC
And some very odd looks from the neighbors
When we had Auntie Ethel for tea.

It was Sunday and people were coming
There were fifteen expected you see
We were stuck for a main course to give them
So we had Auntie Ethel for tea.

There were peas, there were sprouts
There were chips all about
But the big treat they had to agree
Was the medium rare guest of honor
When we had Auntie Ethel for tea.

Now there's some folks like food cooked Italian
And there's some like their food Chinee
But I'm proud to say we all ate British
When we had Auntie Ethel for tea.

The police took us away and I'm sorry to say
With our cooking they didn't agree
Though we promised them that was the last time
That we'd have Auntie Ethel for tea.

YOU ALWAYS EAT
THE ONE YOU LOVE
Kim Newman

You always eat the one you love,
The one you shouldn't munch at all,
You always take the sweetest rose,
And chew it till the petals fall,
You always gulp the kindest heart,
For that tasty snack you can't recall,
So if I ate your heart last night,
That's because I love you most of all . . .

CHOCOLATE
AND WORMS
David Garnett

"Eat up your dinner, darling,"
Said the raven to her chick.
"But mummy dear, I hate it.
Worms only make me sick.
Please let me have some chocolate;
Just a taste, one lick."

But Edgar, the baby raven,
Never got his wish.
All he ever ate was worms,
Piled high upon his dish.

Worms for breakfast, worms for lunch,
Worms for supper, and worms for tea.
Edgar grew up big and strong
And went to live in a tree.

"Eat up your dinner, darling,"
His mum told little John.
"Lots of meat and spuds and greens
Will make you big and strong."
"No," said he, and shook his head.
"This meal is all quite wrong.

What I want is chocolate:
That is my favorite treat."
His mother did as she was asked.
(The poor boy had to eat.)

Little John ate nothing else;
He stayed both small and quiet,
The product of consuming
A totally chocolate diet.

Edgar slumbered in his nest,
While children played beneath.
One such child was little John,
Whose bladder sought relief.
For the sake of modesty,
He stepped behind a leaf.

The raven dreamed of chocolate,
The boy unzipped his flies.
Edgar yawned and stretched and stared,
He couldn't believe his eyes.

Small and quiet, John stood no chance.
Edgar screeched out "Caw!"
Big and strong, the bird swooped down . . .
Little John was no more.

John survived the raven's beak,
But never was the same.
Taken to the hospital,
He later changed his name.
Wearing ribbons and a dress,
He's known as little Jane.

Edgar's wish now had come true,
The memory to savor.
A tasty, chewy, wriggly worm,
Chocolate was its flavor.

The moral of this story, kids,
Is really very easy:
Always eat your dinner up,
And be careful where you wee wee.

THE DANGERS
OF COLOR TV
Simon Ian Childer

When I'm sitting watching telly,
I like to pick holes in my belly.
And when I've got enough of those,
I fill them with snot from up my nose.
The hole God gave me's got a knot in.
I cannot get a lot of snot in.

THE CHILDREN'S HOUR

Alan Moore

There were no video nasties in my disadvantaged youth
On which to slake my budding thirst for grue:
Mother held that blood was ghastly and that entrails were
   uncouth
And decapitation not the thing to do.
So though I longed for teenagers dismembered in a bog
By some chainsaw-wielding mutant on a spree,
I'd sit and watch the naming of the new *Blue Peter* dog
Via the miracle of children's hour T.V.
I'd gaze as men with soda syphons made each other damp
And stupid brainless puppets misbehaved,
But Sooty was no substitute for *S.S. Torture Camp*
Nor Bengo for *I Spit Upon Your Grave*.
And yet, there, in that tedious televisual terrain
Stood one oasis of morbidity:
The Public Safety Broadcasts! They could petrify the brain
And quite dispel one's appetite for tea.
They spurned the happy images of childhood and instead
Portrayed a world both desolate and grim
Where smoking ruin lay in wait for tots who smoked in bed,
Or weed-choked ponds for those who couldn't swim.
Small children playing happily beside a busy road
Became a prospect tinged with doubt and fear,

As fatherly narrators calmly read the Green Cross Code
Then smashed eggs with a brick to make things clear.
The Unattended Gas-Tap! The Over-Loaded Plug!
The Fridges, where you'd suffocate or freeze!
The Badly-Parked Ice Cream Van and the Treacherous
    Sliding Rug!
What need had I of Dracula with these?
I learned how little was required to cross the River Styx,
How little to be rendered dead and gone;
One partly-senile relative and twenty Number Six,
A horse-hair sofa, and a box of Swan.
Above all else, I learned that other people were the snares
On which one's brief balloon might soon be popped.
They failed to dip their headlights or left skateboards on
    the stairs,
Or opened doors on trains before they'd stopped.
I've heard of those who say that viewing horrors as a lad
Will lead to complications late in life,
But speaking for myself I'd say I've not turned out too bad;
I have two children and a lovely wife.
I keep them in the cellar, where the walls are nice and soft,
Preventing sudden falls from causing harm.
They're padded with the stuff I use to insulate the loft;
So far, at least, it's working like a charm.
We don't go out, or walk about. We seldom even stand.
We boil our water twice before we drink.
My childhood terrors caused no lasting damage, Life is grand,
And me and mine are safe at last.

I think.

RADIO NASTY
Stephen Gallagher

Don't watch television. It's bad for your eyes.
They'll swell up to three times their usual size.
Your hands will start shaking, your nose will sprout warts,
And the zits on your bottom will glow through your shorts.
Avoiding these awful effects is fantasti
Cally easy; just listen to Radio Nasty.

Our manager drinks, our presenters all swear.
Our program controller has *things* in his hair.
He calls them his pets and he puts them in boxes,
From where they escape after picking the locks. Is
Our signal unclear or our content too ghastly?
Why *won't* more kids listen to Radio Nasty?

The source of our DJ's best jokes is no mystery,
To anyone well-versed in mankind's pre-history.
We copy the programs the big stations do;
We steal all our news from the newspapers, too.
If our weatherman thinks it will be overcast, he
Tells lies about sunshine on Radio Nasty.

Why don't people like us? Why won't they tune in?
We seem as well-liked as a cold custard-skin.

But we've phone-ins and quizzes on most afternoons,
And a few of our jingles have even got tunes.
No need to have fears about being outclassed, we
Won't stretch your IQ here on Radio Nasty.

Examples; a program on toads being pickled,
And laughalong records of nuns being tickled.
Advice should your granny sprout fangs and grow hairy
And start to dismember the Christmas-tree fairy.
A typical recipe's live cockroach pasty
In Cookery Corner on Radio Nasty.

Guessword competitions are cheap and they're fun;
There's only one answer, and that's always "bum".
Write in on a postcard, win wonderful prizes
Like used paper hankies in three different sizes.
What's wrong with our output? It can't differ vastly
From others doing better than Radio Nasty.

Forget all your comics. Forget all your books.
You'll squint from the eyestrain and ruin your looks.
Your hair will fall out and your legs turn unsteady —
I've warned you of these kinds of danger already.
Let one entertainment that can't be surpassed be
A tranny, a sick-bag, and Radio Nasty.

SOMETHING CAME OUT OF THE TOILET

Harry Adam Knight

Something came out of the toilet,
Slimy and shiny and thick.
It looked like a gelatinous drainpipe
And smelled quite distinctly of sick.

It had some sort of hole at its top end
Like a mouth or a hollowed-out eye
Or a nostril that maybe it ate with
Or an ear through which it might spy.

A glistening liquid came from it
That might have been poison, or not,
But then it could well have been tears
Or a trickle of luminous snot.

I should really have run away shouting
But instead I stayed very still too.
I just stood on the landing and watched it,
Wondering what it would do.

My patience was quickly rewarded
And I might add my courage as well
(though it might have been only sheer terror
That held me transfixed, who can tell?).

The oozing black creature moved forward,
Slithering over the seat.
My heart leaped like a frog on a hot plate
As it crawled just an inch from my feet.

But it didn't do anything to me
As I stood in the quiet and gloom.
It seemed to know where it was going,
And that was my parents' room.

Its head disappeared through the doorway
And its tail — well, I just don't know.
It might still have been in the sewer
Among all that brown stuff, below.

I thought that I ought to do something
Instead of just standing still,
So I followed it quietly, quickly
And what I saw made me feel ill.

The black creature's single damp orifice
Was attached to the side of the head
Of my father who seemed to be sleeping
In the duvet-warm comfort of bed.

But sleep was just inconceivable
In view of what I could hear,
For the noises of slobber and slurping
Meant it was sucking his brain through his ear.

)With a sudden slight gasp and convulsion
My dad's head appeared to deflate
As the creature moved back from its sucking
With a grey lump it hurriedly ate.

Before I could take any action
It moved with its mouth open wide
And repeated the whole grisly business
Around at my mother's side.

When its feast was apparently over
I wondered if *my* time had come.
If not me there was only the tom cat
And a parrot that had a sore bum.

But the creature was obviously sated
For it slowly began to retreat
Back into the cold smelly water
Under the lavatory seat.

For a moment it stood there all rigid
As I watched, hardly daring to blink.
And it seemed, just before it sank downwards
That its orifice gave me a wink.

In the stillness I sat and I wondered
What would be the best thing to do.
I knew that I ought to tell someone
But I wasn't exactly sure who.

I finally decided the police force
Would not disbelieve a small boy,
Though first, for safety before phoning,
I'd a black magic book to destroy . . .

THE SECRET
BOOK OF THE DEAD
Terry Pratchett

They don't teach you the facts of death,
Your Mum and Dad. They give you pets.
We had a dog which went astray.
Got laminated to the motorway.
I cried. We had to post him to the vet's.

You have to work it all out by yourself,
This dying thing. Death's always due.
A goldfish swimming on a stall,
Two weeks later: cotton wool,
And sent to meet its Maker down the loo.

The bottom of our garden's like a morg-you
My Dad said. I don't know why
Our tortoise, being in the know
Buried *himself* three years ago.
This is where the puppies come to die.

Puss has gone to be a better cat
My Dad said. It wasn't fair.
I think my father's going bats
Jesus didn't come for cats
I went and looked. Most of it's still there.

They don't teach you the facts of death,
Your Mum and Dad. It's really sad.
Pets, I've found, aren't built to last;
One Christmas present, next Christmas past.
We go on buying them. We must be mad.

They die of flu and die of bus,
Die of hardpad, die of scabies,
Foreign ones can die of rabies,
But usually they die of us.

MUMMY'S BLOCKED
THE LAV AGAIN
John Grant

Mummy's blocked the lav again:
She only does it now and then,
When she gets "just slightly tight",
Then cooks and cooks all through the night,
Her eyes filled with arcane delight —
Her micro filled with Ken.

> *Ken, Ken, poor old Ken,*
> *Just like all her other men*
> *Grew rather boring when alive,*
> *So, goodbye, Daddy 25.*

Bigger bits go down the drain,
The cat enjoys the coddled brain,
Some bits Mummy likes to save,
But some parts get a "wat'ry grave":
Now from the lav his fingers wave
As on the flush we strain.

> *Ken, Ken, poor old Ken,*
> *Just like all her other men*
> *Most goes down, but some bits stick —*
> *Now, who'll be Daddy 26?*

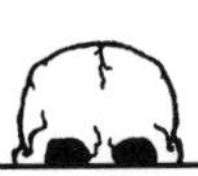

In Loving Memory

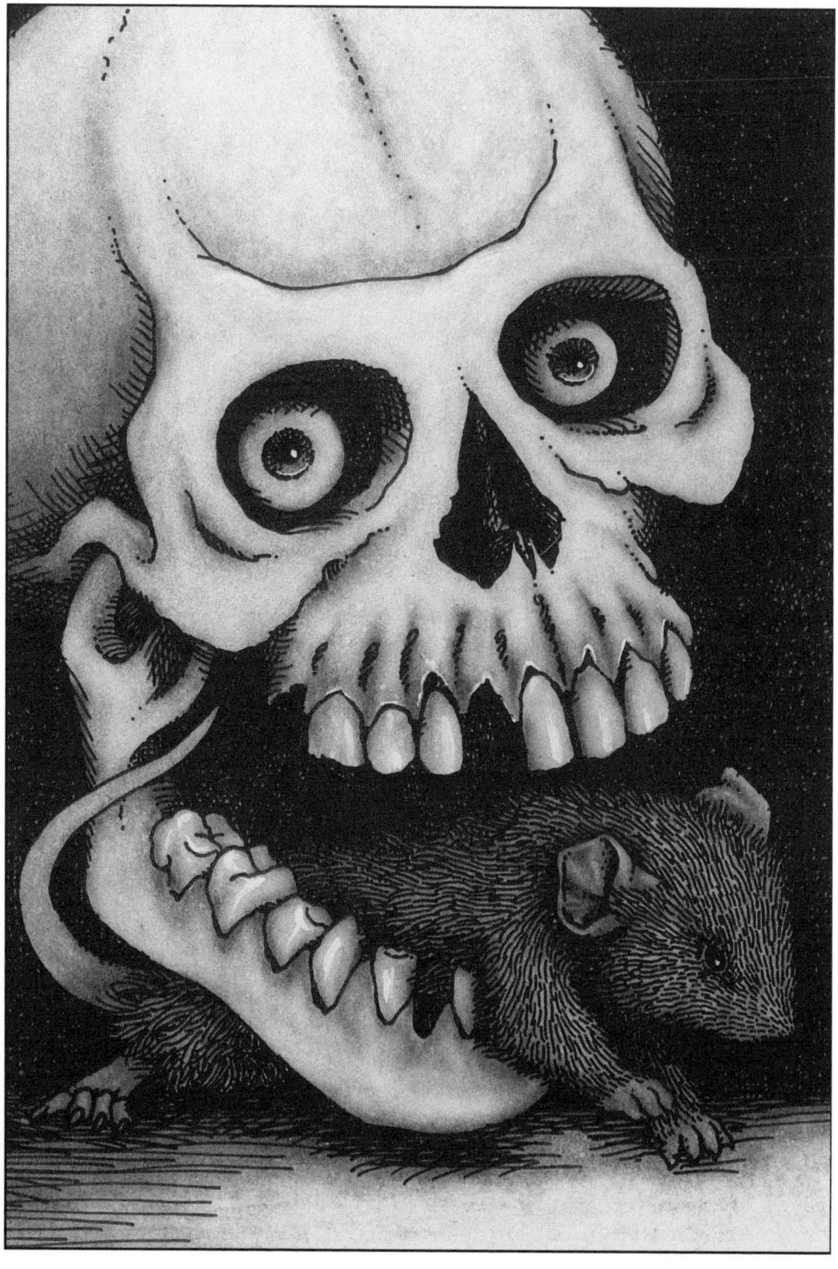

RICE PUDDING

Brian Aldiss

(after A.A. Milne)

What is the matter with Mary Jane?
We hospital doctors stand round and complain
That the blip on her VDU's going insane.
What is the matter with Mary Jane?

What is the matter with Mary Jane?
We've analyzed all her intestines contain
(Diced carrot, black pudding and chinese chow mein)
What is the matter with Mary Jane?

What is the matter with Mary Jane?
We've sunk our electrodes down into her brain;
I've tried two catheters, I've tried to explain.
  But her bloody relations are weeping again . . .

What is the matter with Mary Jane?
Among other things she has pre-menstrual pain.
(I guess that by now you'll recall the refrain:
What is the matter with Mary Jane?)

Where, by the way, is Mary Jane?
A nurse has already cracked under the strain:
The toilets and bedpans are filling in vain,
Where, by the way, is Mary Jane?

Who, incidentally, is Mary Jane?
She was nude when they carried her in from the rain.
Her driving license was issued in *Spain* . . .
Who, incidentally, is Mary Jane?

What is the matter with Mary Jane?
She seems to want someone to entertain —
Phone Kylie Minogue or perhaps Michael Caine.
> *Now her bloody relations are weeping again* . . .

What is the matter with Mary Jane?
We've tried a heart transplant, X-rays, and methane,
And all the rest of the legerdemain.
What is the matter with Mary Jane?

What is the matter with Mary Jane?
I'll bet you my scalpel her life's on the wane —
She tried a U-turn in the M4 fast lane.
> *And her bloody relations are weeping again* . . .

THE GOOD SHIP
"REVENGER",
Or, What the Crew Don't Know Won't Hurt Me

(writ anonymously by) Galad Elflandsson
(with inspiration by George MacDonald Fraser)

I don't know a damn thing about tops'ls
Or mains'ls an' stays'ls or what
An' I ain't never been on the high seas afore
Nor wreaked murder wi' powder an' shot.

So Heaven knows why I'm Black Bart's cabin b'y
On this rum-soaked black barque bound for Hell
But it don't take much brights, when out go the lights
T'know somethin', in the bilges, doth smell.

The Captain's a fine 'un fer fleerin'
At Spaniards an' Frenchies an' such
With "Begad!" an' "Belike!" he gives 'em the spike
An' then smacks in their skulls wi' his crutch.

But lately I been noticin' he's uneasy
Tho' there's buckets o' gold in the hold
An' silver an' spice, an' great jewels o' price
Still the Cap'n's been actin' a bit cold.

So's I asked him about the bilges, I said,
As we stood off the Windwards one night
"Oh Cap'n we're made, like King Charlie's own jade
But there's somethin' belowdecks ain't right!"

Then Bart gave a start, wi' a belch an' a fart
An' he whacked the ship's parrot fer good measure
"What the hell d'ye mean?" he said, turnin' a mite green
"There's nothin' down there but the treasure!"

"God help us!" I said, wi' a shake o' me head
"But there's more'n just timbers an' swag
In the bilges last night, I seen eyes blinkin' bright
An' a chill at me innards didst nag . . ."

"The de'il ye say!" sez Bart turnin' grey
As he turned for a swig o' his toddy
"Ha' ye been at the rum, ye snotty wee scum,
Or are ye plain goin' half-wit an' noddy?"

"No no, sir," sez I, trotters ready t'fly
As he looked t'be gettin' sore angered
"I'm certain I seen 'em, great peepers a sheenin'
An' teeth champin' I wot, or I'm hangered!"

Then Bart put his hand on me shoulder belikes
An' he grinned an' he simpered real sickly
An' he poured us a tot which he drank like a shot
Afore he turned back t'me right quickly.

"Laddie," sez he, "mind close-like t'me
An' mayhap ye'll l'arn somethin' worth knowin'
For yer share's down below, an' likely t'grow
If some good sense ye're mindful o' showin' . . ."

So's I drunk down me drink, all mummed by his wink
An' repaired me t'bed all a-shakin'
For I know'd Bart real good, as his cabin b'y should
An' fer damn sure I know'd he warn't fakin'.

Now I'm snoozled wi' rum, playin' blind deaf an' dumb
An' so what if I'm damned for a sinner
The crew's gettin' smaller, but my pile's gettin' taller
An' that sure as hell beats bein' dinner.

THE DREAM
OF OMAR K. YAM
Maliciously Rendered Into English Verse
by David Sutton

"Awake! The morning licks the dreamer's night
And spits upon your eyes like sister's spite:
Lo — the Bogey-Man of our dreams has slobbered
For your soul, and lost it with the honeyed light."

Up from dream's centre through the veil
Omar rose, the boy; and on the throne did wail:
And many slimy, groping serpents by his smelly feet did slither,
But awaken or die, dismay'd, Omar could do neither.

He dreamt that in and out, about, below,
'tis nought but nightmare's Shadow-Show,
Acted out in candle-light of mind,
Round which phantom regurgitations come and go!

Eating worms and earwigs caught in terror,
Was oft the phlegmy content of that mind's aether:
But lo! This night the carapace and pus of insects
Was gone, and in its place even worse a horror.

And when the dawn with shining sun did vent
His bedroom and he awake, Omar still dreamt:
Festooned in gaily-color'd crimson his spiteful sister sat
Not staring, still: Her body from its clotted head was rent!

YOU'RE DECEASED,
FATHER WILLIAM

Colin Greenland

(After Lewis Carroll)

"You're deceased, Father William," the young man said,
"And your skin has become very green.
But you stroll down the boulevard toting your head:
Don't you think this is a trifle obscene?"

"In my youth," grinned the spectre, "I read many books
By Campbell and Barker and King
Which convinced me that lipless, cadaverous looks
were demonstrably *every* year's thing."

"You're extinct," said the youth. "One can tell this because
Squishy maggots inhabit your bones.
Black fungus erupts where your larynx once was.
Whence issue these sepulchral groans?"

"My dialogue coach," croaked the separate head,
"Is an expert from Hollywood, isn't he?
He worked on *Gore 2* and *Divine Meets the Dead*
And reanimated Walt Disney."

"You're defunct," said his junior, "starting to bloat;
Your flesh is no longer intact.
Yet you ravish young maidens and sometimes a goat.
How might one account for this act?"

"In my life," said the skull with an osseous smirk,
"I watched video nasties on loan.
Now nightmares they gave me persist in the murk:
I'm frightened to sleep on my own."

"But you're dead," stressed his interlocutor. "I beg,
Father William, return to your grave.
Your funeral cost us an arm and a leg.
This really is no way to behave."

"In my death," howled the zombie, "I eat many brains
Which I scoop from their shells with my claws.
You can write the expense off as capital gains.
Be off! or I'll breakfast on yours."

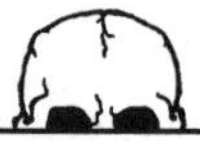

Less Welcome Tenants

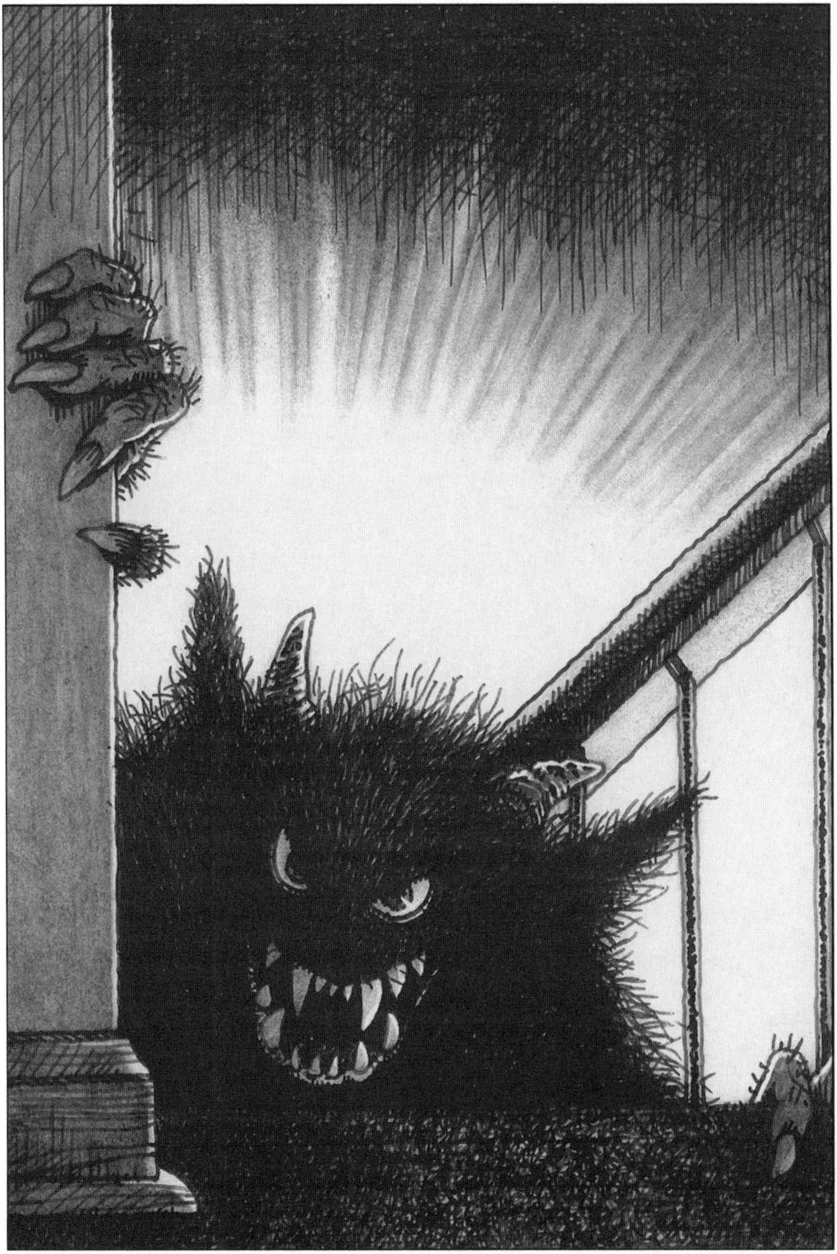

A LANDLADY'S LAMENT

Ramsey Campbell
(for Tammy and Matty)

I never heard of such a thing!
What must he think of me?
Our newest guest in such a state,
and me not dressed for tea!
Now, never mind all hiding.
I know you all can hear.
You needn't think I'm playing
hide and seek again, no fear!
This used to be a decent house.
I'd guests who'd stayed for years.
Until the night the first of you
came up the cellar stairs.
I've always said it isn't how
a person looks that matters.
I never would have thrown you out
like that, all bones and tatters.
But couldn't you have stayed down there?
It's where you like to be.
Instead you drove out all my guests
by sitting down to tea.
When you saw how upset I was
you tried to make amends.

You filled up all my rooms again
by bringing in your friends.
They did their best to cheer me up
with all their little tricks,
him crouching in the firewood
pretending to be sticks,
then scuttling up the chimney
and down the outside wall,
and peering upside down at me
though he'd no face at all.
Her who'd hang above my bed
to wake me in the morning,
and make her eyes roll down her cheeks
if I ever started yawning.
The other one who'd say good morning
shyly round the door,
then sag until his head was spread
across my bedroom floor.
I do appreciate the ways you try
to keep me company.
I just wish sometimes I'd one guest
a little more like me.
That's why I saved one room to let
and kept the notice showing.
Which brought poor Mr. Wintle here
the night that it was snowing.
It wasn't much to ask you all,
to keep out of his way.
He was shy, but he'd have chatted,
and I wanted him to stay.

But no, you had to say hello,
at least those that can speak.
You even shook him by the hand.
When he began to shriek
and run, and try to find the door,
you made sure that he'd stay,
as if I'd meant him just to sit
at table night and day.
And now you've got him in this state,
I'm not at all amused.
He's still our newest guest, you know and
I won't have him abused.
I want him sitting properly
before I serve the meal.
I know you like to play with him,
but I never thought you'd steal.
Just put back everything you took.
You've started my head hurting.
I see where someone's got his legs —
that's them behind the curtain.
And put them back the right way round!
I'm in no mood for japes.
Stop playing with his head at once!
You're like a pack of apes!
That's right, make sure it won't fall off.
And now, what do you do?
Apologize to him and me,
and I should think so too.

Now you'll have to wait for dinner,
and I want no noise at all.
Then if you'll just behave yourselves
I may get you a ball
so that you'll leave our guest alone.
Now, that's my final word.
I've wasted half the evening.
It really is absurd.
Now then, let's make up and be friends,
and when our dinner's done,
let's try to have what I like best:
a nice quiet time at home.

THE BORGIA BRATS

Garry Kilworth

O, Rose you are sick
And so is our Fred:
Willie's still ill
And Jonathon's dead:

It's all happened since
Those kids came today —
Little Lucrezia
And young Cesare.

Invited along
To today's birthday treat,
The Borgia kids brought
Italian sweets:

A black currant pie
That Lucrezia made
Had bright little berries
Of various shades

And colorful mushrooms
Cesare found
Went into a patè
Which we passed around.

"No thank you, kind sir,"
Said polite little sis.
"Nor me," said her brother,
"I'll give it a miss."

Green jellies, black trifles,
Flecked peaches and cream,
And a pudding that hissed
A yellowish steam —

O, Rose had convulsions
And Fred burst his spleen,
While Cesare smiled
At Lucrezia, serene.

It's all happened since
Those kids came today —
Jonathon dead
And the rest, turning grey.

Another
Cursed House Story
(or) Always Enquire About the Prior Tenants
John M. Ford

There's a house with an ill reputation,
There's a room where you'd better not go,
With an unhealthy taste for its tenants
And a Something that dwells far below.

The thing was in the ground when humankind was in the trees.
It watched their race evolve with an amused and vague unease;
It snickered when they stumbled and It giggled when they fell,
And when they took up arms, why then It knew that all was well.
A human hurt another, It delighted in the taste;
A human slew another, and It gorged upon the waste.
Consuming passion, blood, and death, and battening on pain,
It lived and was well nourished on the ancient curse of Cain.
But meals came far apart and accidental — till the day
The humans built a house upon the soil in which It lay.

There's a puddle of blood in the parlor,
There's a body stone dead in the hall,
And belowstairs somebody is screaming,
And Something's enjoying it all.

The builder was a baron, in the year the Normans won,
Who gave service at an altar that was never shown the sun.
He died (and not in bed) and was succeeded by his heir,
Who had an extra limb that grew (I shouldn't mention where).
For centuries the family made sure that It was fed,
(Although despite Its promises, they always wound up dead).
And when (through long inbreeding and the stake) their line
        did fail,
Their "fine ancestral home" was offered up for public sale.
The tenants came and went (mostly went mad). It found this nice,
For meals became monotonous without a little spice.

     The windows are shuttered and dusty,
     The gardens are strangled with weed,
     The cobwebs hang thick from the ceiling,
     And Something is eager to feed.

The Realty agent scans the map, and pouts a bit, and thinks;
His Secretary brings him morning coffee. As he drinks,
He pats her on the backside (as a brother pats a sis)
And says "We just can't rent old Horror Hall. The trouble is,
It's gotten such a rep for gloomy ghastlies in the dark,
I think we ought to knock it down and build an auto park."
He never sees the light that's in his Secretary's eyes,
The paper knife she's holding pierces him with stark surprise.
The Secretary works for the remainder of the day,
And files her late employer under D. and O. and A.

There are boards coming down from the windows,
There's a car being parked in the drive,
There are sounds of unpacking and cleaning,
And Something long dead is alive.

WAITING...
James Herbert

So here I lie beneath the bed
One eye upon the clock
The other's somewhere close by too
Wrapped in a smelly sock.
An arm, I think is in the loo
Next to the toilet cleaner
The fingers make a scouring brush
'Though lately they've worn leaner.
A leg is in the wardrobe
Still in its leather boot
The other's a draft excluder
I'd protest but my tongue is mute.
A hand has become an ashtray
On the dusty mantelshelf
The fingers curled hold cigarettes
(Remember, these are bad for health!)
My torso's over there, sitting in a wicker
No arms, no legs, no head, no life
Can you imagine anything sicker?
Also absent is my heart
Spleen, kidneys, and liver too
By now I expect you've already guessed
Just who likes meaty stew.
The only blessing I suppose —
And this might make you think —

I'd hate the smell of rotting flesh
But my nose is in the sink.
So here my head lies in the dark
Listening with half an ear
Those nibbling maggots at my brain
Will soon stop thoughts I fear.
And here he comes, that crazed axeman
All chuckles and sniggers and leers
To put me all together again —
Christ! This could go on for years.

THE THING AT THE
TOP OF THE STAIRS
Sharon Baker

Something lives at the top of the stairs:
Teeth, a smell of dead parsley and feet,
The sound of cats mewing. I hide in my sheet
Quaking like jelly eclairs.

Something squeals at the top of the stairs
Under my door roll plumes and a carrot
Mew, belch. My white rabbit. Oh, no. And the parrot!
"Fill up on *them*," go my prayers.

Something grows at the top of the stairs
From the poodle, a yip; From the manx, a squall
Mew, splat! A gobbet of flesh hits the wall
On the rug: brains, feathers, and hairs.

"Something bad's at the top of the stairs!"
"Nonsense." Mom takes up the clothes. "Eat your lox."
Mew, shriek! Down slithers her nose with the socks.
At breakfast, just one, not two chairs.

"Something grabbed Mom at the top of the stairs!"
Dad drops his suitcase. "I'll check it out, fella."
Mew, munch! Down rains his bloody umbrella,
Visa card, cash, and bus fares.

Who feeds the thing at the top of the stairs?
I do. I say, "My folks went to Des Moines.
Want to see my new Walkman, boom box, Dad's gold coins?
That mew? Just the cat. After you!"

THINGS THAT
GO BUMP IN
THE NIGHT

Ian Pemble
(for Hayley and Robert)

Let's drink a toast
To the study of ghosts
And things that go bump in the night,
For the ghastly phenomena
Of these goings on're a
Source of intrigue and delight.

Now some think my mission
To track apparitions
As dull as ditchwater — or duller.
But their size and dimensions,
Their astral pretentions
Never pall — and they're often in color!

In Brighton and Hove
They're frightfully mauve,
They're rustically russet in Notts. ,
You'll find they're tartan
In parts of Dunbarton.
In Paisley they've, strangely, got spots.

The ghosts around Bude
Are invariably nude.
Is this rude? No, it's merely transparent.
They have strips down their sides
In the Outer Hebrides,
But in Hampshire, near Havant, they haven't.

I've been on their trails
Throughout England and Wales,
In the Lands of the Spud and the Sporran.
Though my investigative
Reports concern natives,
I *have* met a few who are foreign.

One ghost on a train
Left appalling red stains.
Was this blood? Or was I being foolish?
Then I cried out, "Eureka!
I've got it — Paprika.
Of course, a Hungarian ghoulish!"

I've hunted for specters
Over millions of hectares,
And I must say I rather *like* ghosts.
They don't leave a mess,
Never talk to the Press,
And eat children scrambled on toast.

Before they prepare them
They giggle and scare them,
And tickle them nightly and daily.
Then these horrible monsters
Sit down to grilled youngsters . . .
Preferably Roberts and Hayleys!

Ah, those were the days . . .
But I'm sorry to say
They're becoming quite feeble and gaunt.
There used to be hosts
But they gave up the ghost
And are not seen around their old haunts.

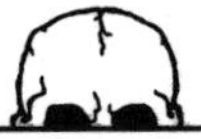

Night Fears

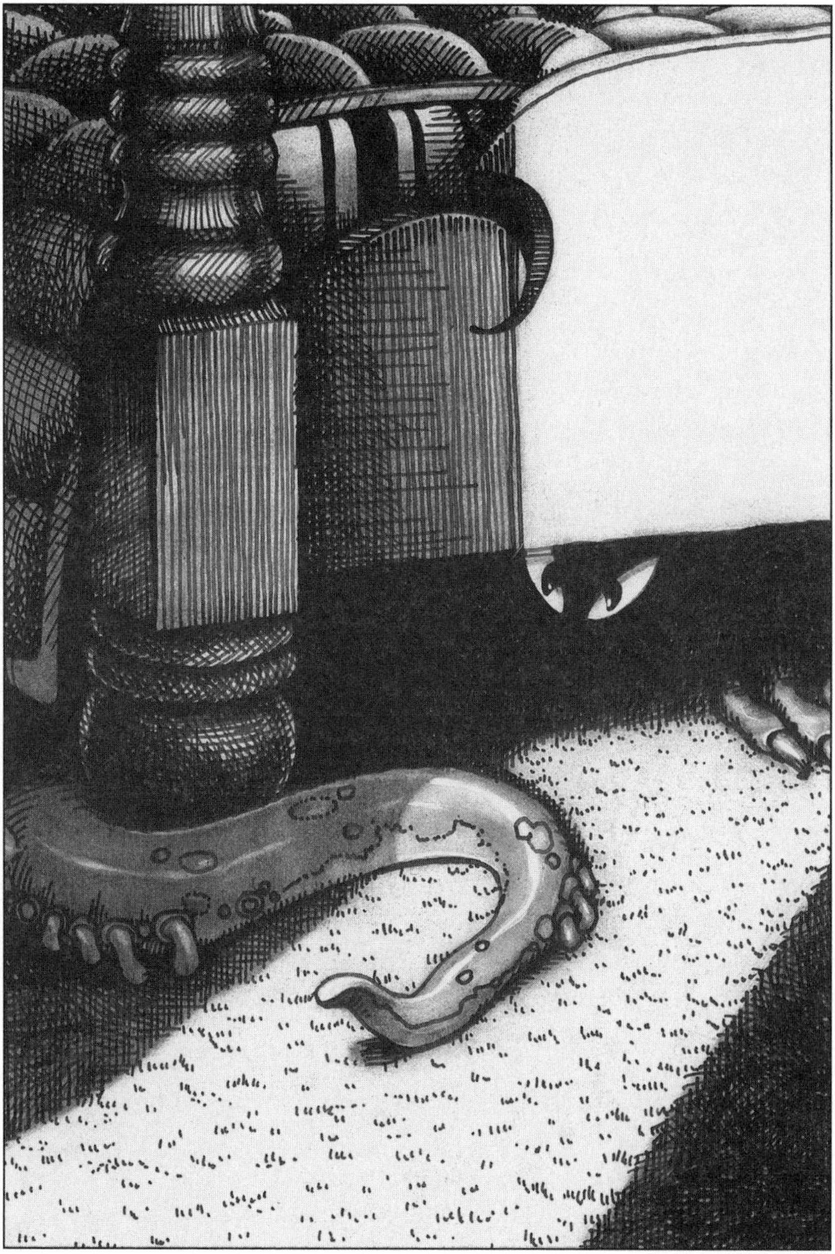

IN THE DARK
Storm Constantine

From reading tales of charnel gods
And watching nasty vids,
There comes a time, oh sweetling brat,
Most loathed by every kid.

To mount the creaking stair by dark,
to pass black, open doors;
Nighttime beckons, little one,
To settle somber scores.

Beneath the bed, a creature lurks,
With fiery tongue and loathsome nose.
It waits with tentacles atwitch,
For sweet uncovered hands and toes.

Lights off and down beneath the quilt,
You burrow, child of trembling heart,
To listen to the shadows hiss,
The faintest tremor in the dark.

Is it *really* creeping claws
That drag across the carpet thread?
Is it *really* sucking breath
Coming from beneath the bed?

What demon is it lifts the sheet
To mischief cheerfully disposed?
What evil foulness reaching out
For flesh nocturnally exposed?

Helpless, sleepless, tense you lie,
Waiting for the clammy paw,
Mother, father never come,
Like exorcism at the door.

"Mum, I never called you thick,
It was a lie my sister said.
Dad, I never made a fuss
Or when you thumped me, wished you dead . . ."

Gently rasping, monsters stir,
Shifting foulness, rot and fat.
Is their purpose to annoy
Or worse, chastise, a wilful brat?

"I'll be good tomorrow, Mum,
Wash dishes, clean behind my ears,
Promise, honest; I'll be *good*,
'Cos now I need you. COME IN HERE!"

Can't they hear the muffled snarls
From their room across the hall?
In the morning, when they wake
Will you still be here *at all* . . . ?

LIGHTS OUT
Alex Stewart

Little boy shivers alone in the night,
And hides under blankets, heart pounding with fright,
Stilling his breathing as much as he dares —
For Something Unpleasant is creeping upstairs.

A creak on the landing — the give of a joist?
Or the footfall of something that's clammy and moist?
Are the scuffling sounds from the night-shadowed pane
Made by flesh-hungry ghouls, or the wind and the rain?

And from out in the garden, that spine-chilling howl —
Somebody's dog, or a wolf on the prowl?
Is it mice in the skirting that scrabble and squeak,
Or the souls of the damned as they suffer and shriek?

Do demons and witches still ride through the night,
Cocooned in the darkness and shunning the light?
Is it really a pigeon that scrapes on the roof,
Or the sulphurous scratching of Lucifer's hoof?

The house breathes around him like something alive,
Allowing his terrors to blossom and thrive,
And the specters that whisper their way through the door
Chill the child to the bone as they blow round the floor.

Little boy shivers alone in the night,
Until terrors dissolve with the dawn's gentle light —
And Something Unwholesome, of shadows and dread,
Creeps away down the stairs, now contented and fed.

A MOTHER'S TENDER LOVE
Jo Fletcher

Bethany, Bethy child,
Innocent maid,
Can you not tell where you've been?
Huddled alone with no hope in your eyes —
And not even able to scream . . .

Bethany, Bethy child,
Golden-haired girl,
Can you not hint where you've run?
Tresses entangled, curls ripped and torn
Like hell-hounds pursued you — and won.

Bethany, Bethy child,
Piteous pale,
Can you not voice what was said?
Your young hands are clenched up in impotent fear
Your wild eyes are frantic with dread.

Bethany, Bethy child,
Corpse-pallored babe,
Now you are orphan no more.
Ah, don't pull away with such terror-glazed mien
From a mother who loves you so sore.

Bethany, Bethy child,
Dear daughter mine,
Why don't you smile and be gay?
Your mother has come back from so very far,
Come back to take you away.

Bethany, Bethy child,
Frail young thing,
Why do you hopelessly moan?
When I have travelled from death — and beyond.
I've come to take you . . . home.

CATCAWLS
Samantha Lee

On Wild wintry evenings,
When stormclouds are whipped,
You might see a Catcawl
Creep out of a Crypt.
They live in the graveyard
Deep under the stones
In bloodcurdling caverns
Constructed from bones
That eerily echo
With screeches and groans.
They huddle together
Deep under the rime
And they munch moldy marrow
And freshly chilled slime
And eyes — which they polish off
Four at a time.
Beware of the Catcawl
Who's frequently found
By gravediggers working
The freshly tilled ground.
Best to stay in your bed
Huddled under the sheets.
Catcawls stalk in the darkness
Patrolling the streets.

They hide around corners
Where runaways play
To trap the unwary
And steal them away.
"And how will I know them,"
I hear you enquire,
"These Catcawls with habits
So dreath and so dire?"
It's hard to mistake them
When once they've been seen.
Their noses are wormeaten,
Mouths are obscene,
And their ears are like cabbage leaves
Wrinkled and green.
Their teeth are like razors
Stained bloodily red.
They have one eye which sits
On the top of their head.
They're covered in hair.
They're disgustingly fat.
A kind of a cross
'Twixt a frog and a rat
And their breath . . .
Well, their breath has
The stench of the tomb
And their catcalling calls
Like the knelling of doom
As it gloats through the gloaming
And girns in the gloom.
They chuckle and chortle

And cackle in glee
At the prospect of meeting
With you or with me.
So it's best to stay in
When you've finished your tea.
For they prowl through the night-time
Like Vampires, like voles.
And they're not altogether
The kindest of souls.
"But where do they come from,"
You want me to tell,
"These horrible freaks,
It must surely be Hell?"
Well, I couldn't be certain,
It may not be true,
But I have heard it said
Between me, between you,
That Catcawls are children
Who've been very bad
Who're rude to their elders
And drive their Mum's mad
Who spit at the Postman
Who walk on the grass
And stick out their feet
When old ladies go past.
Who don't do their homework
Who don't clean their teeth
And who lift up the carpet
To see what's beneath.

I've heard, though it may be
A tissue of lies,
That children who pinch
All the Christmas mince pies
Are turned into Catcawls
In the dead of the night
And spirited off
Long before it is light
to those damp, hollow hutches
Deep under the ground
And kept there —
'Til two hundred years have turned round.
So if you've been wicked
You'd better watch out.
Make sure you behave
If a Catcawl's about.
For if this story's real,
Yes, suppose it's all *true*,
The next to creep out of the Crypt
Could be *YOU!*

THE HAUNTED
HENHOUSE;
Or The Irate Ghost of Thomas Hood
Jessica Amanda Salmonson

Our mum — who Bess and I found dead
Out back inside the chicken shed
With eyes pecked out and nose pecked blue
In pools of blood and chicken goo —
Was seen today with feeding pail
Of chicken mash. We heard her wail,
"Here chicky-chick." We quaked to watch
Intestines dangle from her crotch
Which chickens took for worms to pick —
"Here chicky-chick. Here chicky-chick."

Tonight, Bess and I, in our bed,
While clinging tightly, head by head,
Observed the ghost of Thomas Hood
Who came to say, "Your poem's no good,"
Then with our mum led by the arm
He took her from the shed and farm
To vanish into sodden skies
Leaving two girls with bulging eyes . . .

"I like those chickens less and less,"
Said Bess to me and I to Bess.

WHEN THE MUSIC
BREAKS
R.A. Lafferty

"Mama, Kirol died just now when he was playing the piano. I know he is dead — I can tell by his eyes. But he keeps on playing after he is dead. Make him stop."

"Oh, let him alone, Alcestis! It's the prettiest I've ever heard him play. And besides, dead people have few enough pleasures as it is."

— *Enniscorthy Chronicle, 1826.*

The City Built to Music nears its term,
(on upright instrument that's ten feet tall.
or is the player-genius rather small?),
It sounds a bit like "Nocturne of the Worm".
One thing is real, The Pinnacles of Hell;
But if you build the music very high
You'll rise above them to the slippery sky
And build a City for a Citadel.
Oh shaky in a tinkle-music sky!
Oh tenuous as is the smell of nard!
Collapsible as any house of cards:
And, should the music snap, we'll fade and die.

The City Built to Music breaks its tune!
(Small hands were never meant to stretch so far).
Like fractured pieces falling from the moon.
Like sudden blood out-spurting from a star.
(Oh, fall like lightning, fall so very far!)

But 'twas a tallish town for several whiles,
With fewer than expected flecks and flakes,
A Blesséd City with a blesséd sound.
Immediately everyone reviles
The shattered carcass, when the music breaks
And rolls in little pieces on the ground.

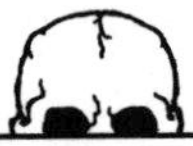

Adults Only

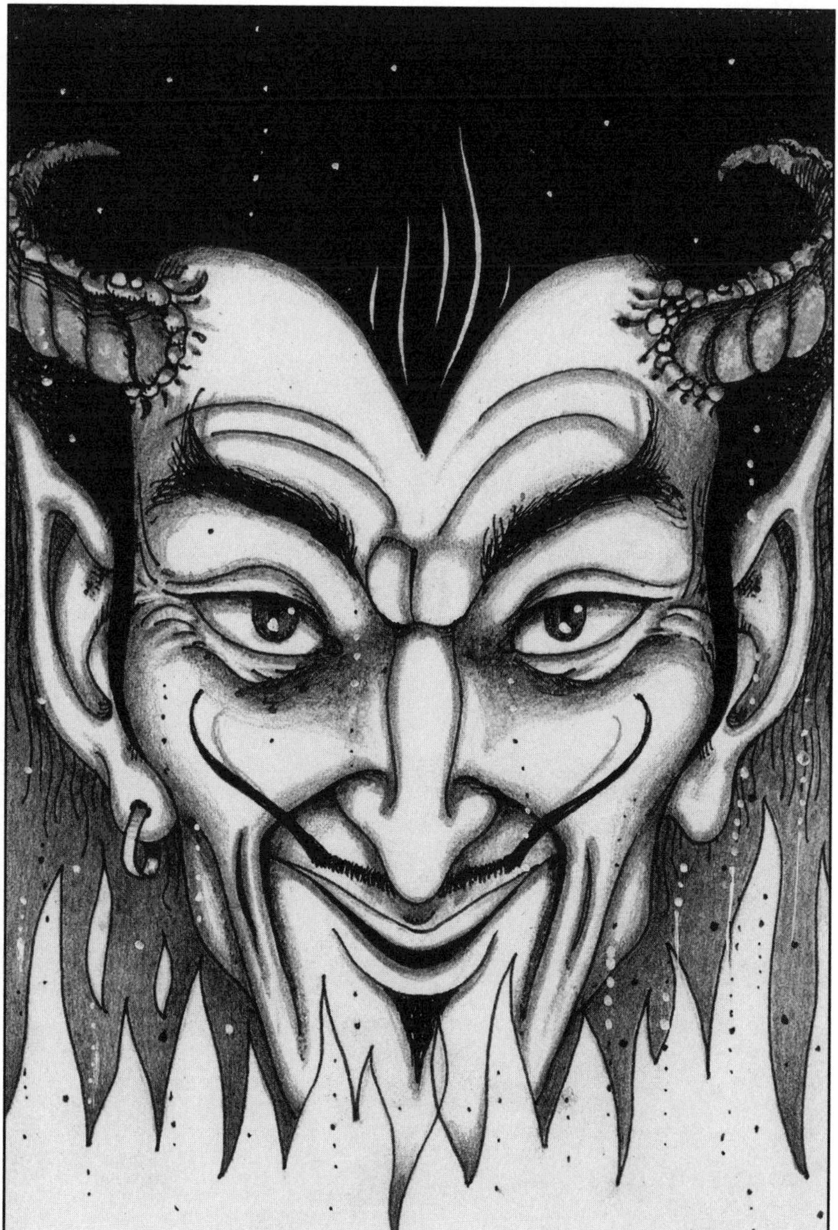

NASTY SNOW
Jody Scott

O how I love to go snorting cocaine
Up in my playroom blue,
Yes I do think it's the loveliest thing
Ever a child could do.

I poisoned my relatives, Mummy and all
With tasty cyanide toddies
Then doused the gazebo with plenty of fuel
And burnt their writhing bodies.

I peddled their cars and hocked all their jewels
Then forged to get Papa's savings,
I sold stylish Sis to a pimp named Bliss
And fed my insatiable cravings.

I bludgeoned sweet Nanny and fingered her stash
For an extra gram of kite,
Now I sit in the buff
And I snuff and I snuff
All through the crystal night

For nothing is finer than snorting 'til dawn
Safe from the cops and the rain,
With the door nailed shut
And the phone wires cut
In a child's own world of cocaine.

WHY PRIVATE WAR
Or, "Why They Pinned
This Name on My Progenitor"
Gene Wolfe

There breathe no dragons anymore,
And throttling bears is such a bore,
It's always soppy at the shore,
And you're too young to get a whore.

Yes, earth seems dull on every score,
And even stealing from the store,
Brings but your weary sigh, "What for?"
Yet wait, O child I adore!
There still remains the secret lore,
That lurks behind the Men's Room door.

There you may learn of *Slaves of Gor,*
The functions of our human spore,
The Hammer of the Great God Thor,
And other things good folks abhore.

And you shall learn, by metaphor,
And scratchings of some gay graffitor,
As o'er those winsome walls you pore.
(I know it well; it I know sore.)

So, little man, learn one thing more.
Add but my number to the corps
— 'tis triple X, XX54 —
And this old hand will spill your gore!
I'll pour your guts out on the floor,
Nor will I like you, furthermore.

L'Envoi
Kid, I'll forgive you well before
You hear the splash of Charon's Oar.
Then great God's mercy I'll implore,
And wrap me in a mantle poor,
Bind rueful brows in mandrigor,
To please the judge and each juror;
Recant like an ambassador,
And break each grave, judicial snore,
With many a penitential roar.

THE ANSWERING
MACHINE

S.P. Somtow

(affectionately dedicated to Robert Bloch)

Oh Mummy dear, I knew you'd call
      To make sure we're all right;
And, if disaster should befall,
      You'd cancel Theatre Night.

You fondly think that girl you hired
      Has shipped us off to bed;
That we've obediently retired,
      Tucked in, our prayers all said.

You must be quite upset to hear
      This brusque machine intone;
The babysitter, though, we fear,
      Can't make it to the phone.

We'd loosen up the ropes and leave
      Un-noosed that shapely nape,
But tightening makes her bosoms heave,
      And Teddy *so* loves rape.

I'm just amazed at Teddy's skill
    At violating virgins;
And at that huge and fleshy drill
    That from his trousers burgeons —

I can't wait till *I* grow a dick!
    It must be very nice,
For now, alas, I have to stick
    To human sacrifice.

It's not that we're that keen to pierce
    With blades that fair complexion;
But that old man with horns looks fierce,
    And brooks no insurrection.

"Old man?" I hear your worried voice,
    "Molesters are a danger!"
But dear Mama, we had no choice,
    Besides, he's not a stranger.

He often visits our boudoir
    A helping hand to lend,
And all the time you thought him our
    Imaginary friend.

It's all your fault you left that book
    Beneath the cookie jar,
And for a school text I mistook
    That leather-bound grimoire.

When I asked Teddy if he might
      Read me a bedtime story,
Our friend breezed in that very night,
      In aspect grim and gory.

At first we asked for simple thrills:
      Huge warts for Peggy Price,
And diarrhea for Marvin Mills,
      And for James Jarvis, lice —

But now our fun has grown complex,
      Our kicks sophisticated,
Our pleasures laced with kinky sex,
      Our violence X-rated.

Wide-eyed I watched dear Teddy flay
      A hapless cat alive:
"Oh, let me skin one too, I pray!"
      "Perhaps when you turn five."

And what of Uncle Pete? Next time
      You're cleaning up the shed,
You'll find, encrusted with dried slime,
      His putrid, severed head.

I don't think Daddy's coming back
      From the conference in Nice;
We nailed him to the railroad track —
      I hope he rests in peace.

You wondered why he lost his ardor
        After his trip to Venice?
We knifed him as he scoured the larder,
        And used his balls for tennis!

Tonight we'll cast this awesome spell,
        And you'll come home to find
Your darling ones enthroned in Hell,
        The contract's just been signed.

There's one condition though, in fact,
        On which these prizes ride;
Your darling cherubs must enact
        A grisly matricide.

The line's gone dead! Where are you, mater?
        Fled the theatre lobby?
Forgetting that you've planned, for later,
        A tryst with Uncle Bobby?

I watch the babysitter's fear,
        I watch her features wilt;
"Yet — *must* we kill our mother dear?"
        I feel a twinge of guilt.

But Teddy's confident reply
        Inspires me to the core;
"It's right and proper that she die —
        Because she is a whore!"

I hear your Volvo pulling up,
      With ecstasy we shiver,
Little you know we soon shall sup
      Upon your brains and liver!

And then — at last — the pact we'll seal,
      With my blood and Ted's semen;
Before your innards can congeal
      We'll join our friend the demon —

He's cackling now, lips dribbling slime,
      Demeanor somewhat soused:
"I've not had such fun since the time
      I carried off poor Faust!"

Foul flames are rising from the floor!
      I'm choking on the smell!
Tridents upraised, we've smashed a door
      Into the heart of Hell!

Is anybody listening?
      Who? Yes? And you? I'm fine —
What? Who? Hello? Can't hear a thing
      With that screaming on the line.

Yes, operator? Yes? Ted reckons
      The switchboard is asleep:
But you can talk for thirty seconds
      After you hear the beep.

Epilogue

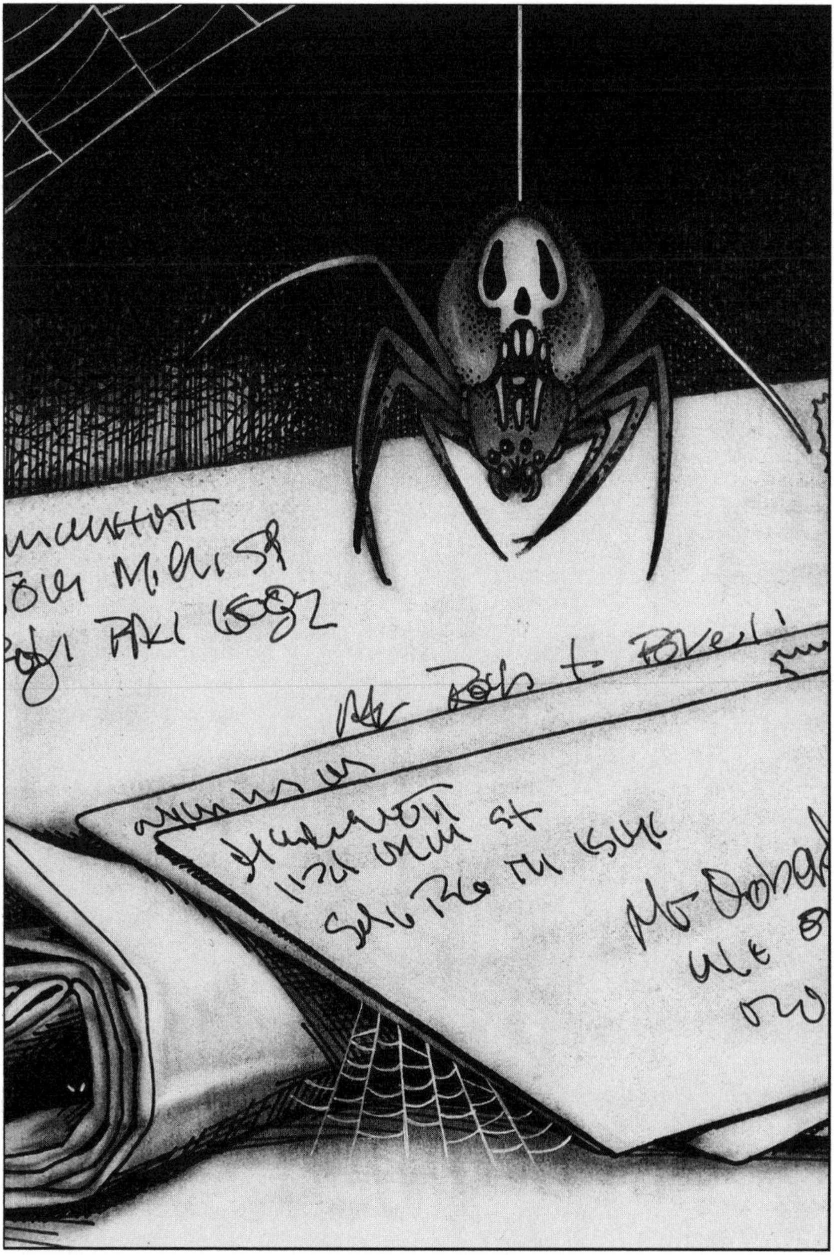

WARNING: DEATH MAY BE INJURIOUS TO YOUR HEALTH

Robert Bloch

When I am dead and buried
It will not matter much
I'll lay there in my coffin
And worms will gnaw my gutch.

My face will melt and vanish
To leave a grinning skull
Though what it has to grin at
I'm sure I cannot tull.

I'll have no mailing address
But postmen soon will learn
To bring me anything that's marked:
"Tomb it may concern."

ABOUT THE EDITORS

Neil Gaiman was told by a school advisor at the age of twelve that it was impossible for him to ever become a comics writer. Since then, he has won every major award you can get in comics (not to mention SF, fantasy and horror). The author of such novels as *Neverwhere*, *American Gods* and *Anansi Boys*, plus award-winning children's books *Coraline*, *The Day I Swapped My Dad for Two Goldfish* and *The Wolves in the Walls*, he has scripted the movies *MirrorMask* and *Beowulf*, and recently made his directing debut with *A Short Film About John Bolton*.

Stephen Jones has written and edited more than eighty books and still can't understand why he's not wealthy. A former television producer/director and genre movie publicist and consultant (the first three *Hellraiser* movies, *Nightbreed* etc.), he is the winner of three World Fantasy Awards, three Horror Writers Association Bram Stoker Awards and three International Horror Guild Awards, as well as being a sixteen-time recipient of the British Fantasy Award and a Hugo Award nominee.

ABOUT THE CONTRIBUTORS

Brian Aldiss has won most of the awards in the international science fiction field: the Hugo, Nebula and John W. Campbell awards from America, the Kurd Lasswitz Award from West Germany, a Jules Verne Award from Sweden and the British Science Fiction Award, while the Australians simply voted him the "World's Best Contemporary Writer of Science Fiction". His autobiography, *The Twinkling of an Eye*, was published in 1998.

Sharon Baker certainly liked to use convoluted titles for her novels: *Quarrelling, They Met the Dragon* was followed by the tongue-twisting *Journey to Membliar* and *Burning Tears of Sassurum*. Her articles and short horror stories appeared in a number of magazines.

Robert ("Psycho") Bloch was saddled with a permanent conjunctive in his name after Alfred Hitchcock took a stab at filming his famous 1959 novel about a boy's love for his Mother. His blend of twisted psychological horror and grim graveyard humor was used to full effect in numerous novels and short stories throughout his long career. *Once Around the Bloch: An Unauthorized Autobiography* was published in 1993.

Ramsey Campbell is described in *The Oxford Companion to English Literature* as "Britain's most respected living horror writer". A multiple award-winner, he has been named Grand Master by the World Horror Convention and received a Lifetime Achievement Award from the Horror Writers Association. Ramsey's most recent novels include *Secret Stories*, *The Overnight* and *The Communications*.

Simon Ian Childer was not a prolific author, but he did have two horror novels published in the 1980s: *Tendrils* was about an invasion of London by acid-spewing alien jellyfish, while *Worm*, about a terrorist plot to incubate a genetically-created species of flesh-eating parasitical worms inside the bodies of young women, was even more popular.

Storm Constantine lives in the British Midlands with her husband and a number of cats. Her novels and stories span the genres of science fiction, fantasy and horror, and she has also written non-fiction titles on the Egyptian zodiac, Ancient Egyptian feline goddesses (with Eloise Coquio) and esoteric psychology (with Deborah Benstead). Her novels include the "Wraeththu" trilogies, while *Silverheart* was a fantasy written with Michael Moorcock.

Galad Elflandsson may sound like a character from Tolkien, but his interest lies in the darker terrors of Ambrose Bierce and Robert W. Chambers. His short fiction has been published in a number of magazines, while his 1979 novel *The Black Wolf*, a Lovecraftian look at lycanthropy, had the distinction of being illustrated by Steve's future brother-in-law.

Jo Fletcher is a poet, writer, critic, journalist and publisher. She won the International Society of Poets' Editors' Choice Award in 1996, the British Fantasy Society's Karl Edward Wagner Award in 1997 and the World Fantasy Award in 2002. Her first poetry collection, *Shadows of Light and Dark* (with an Introduction by Neil) was short-listed for the British Fantasy Award. She is currently Editorial Director of British publisher Gollancz.

John M. Ford is the author of the World Fantasy Award-winning novel *The Dragon Waiting* and the New York Times best-seller *The Scholars of the Night*. He is also the author of two best-selling Star Trek books, *The Final Reflection* and *How Much for Just the Planet?*, but he probably wouldn't want us to mention that.

Stephen Gallagher takes his research very seriously: while in France working on his novel *Oktober*, he managed to gatecrash the security at a Parisian fashion show by showing his Blackburn Library card in lieu of any press credentials. His other books include *Valley of Lights, Down River, White Bizango, The Spirit Box* and *Out of His Mind*. A TV screenwriter and director, he is the creator of the science-and-suspense series *Eleventh Hour*.

David Garnett is a prolific writer of novels and short stories, although much of his work – such as the novelization of *The Hills Have Eyes: Part II* – has been published under a variety of pseudonyms. Books under his own name include *Mirror in the Sky, The Starseekers* and *Time in Eclipse*, while he has edited such anthology series as *The Orbit Science Fiction Yearbook, Zenith* and the 1990s revival of *New Worlds*.

John Grant is a recipient of the Hugo Award, the Locus Award, the World Fantasy Award, the Mythopoeic Society Scholarship Award, as well as a rare British Science Fiction Association Special Award. The author of more than fifty books, both fiction and non-fiction, he co-edited *The Encyclopedia of Fantasy* with John Clute and his numerous other titles include *Masters of Animation* plus *Dragonhenge* and *The Stardragons* (both with Bob Eggleton).

Colin Greenland doesn't often talk about his first novel, *Daybreak on a Different Mountain*, but we thought we'd mention it anyway. His other books include *The Entropy Exhibition, Harm's Way* and *Take Back Plenty*. These days he is most often to be seen on television in the company of his partner Susanna Clarke, author of the best-selling *Jonathan Strange & Mr. Norrell*.

James Herbert is Britain's most successful commercial horror writer, with more than 50 million copies of his books sold worldwide, translated into over thirty languages. In 1974, with the publication of his first novel *The Rats*, they had to create the description "nasties" to describe his work. These days he is the author of such acclaimed best-sellers as *Fluke, The Magic Cottage*,

Haunted and *Nobody True*. However, he still likes to give his readers a scare.

Richard Hill admits to having a somewhat prosaic biography ("Nothing about decorations for bravery, dragging babies from burning buildings or the like."). His poems have been read on the stage, TV and radio and widely published around the world. In 1978 he was awarded the Felicia Hemans Prize for Lyrical Poetry at the University of Liverpool.

Diana Wynne Jones has been enchanting young readers (and adults) with her tales of witches, wizards and warlocks since long before anyone had ever heard of Harry Potter. A winner of the Guardian Award in 1977, her many books include *The Ogre Downstairs*, *The Spellcoats*, *Charmed Life*, *Archer's Goon* and *A Sudden Wild Magic*. Her 1986 novel *Howl's Moving Castle* was turned into a hit animated film by Hayao Miyazaki in 2004.

Garry Kilworth decided to publish his horror novel *The Street* ("The black tarmac is boiling for revenge . . .") under the pseudonym "Garry Douglas", the pen-name he also used for the novelization of *Highlander*. A winner of the World Fantasy Award and the British Science Fiction Award, he was elected a Fellow of the Royal Geographical Society for furthering the knowledge of "historical geography" in his epic trilogy *The Navigator Kings*.

Harry Adam Knight was a well-known figure in British horror and drinking circles. His first novel, *Slimer*, was about a group of shipwreck survivors stalked by a genetically-engineered shape-shifter. It was followed by *The Fungus* (scientifically-engineered mushroom spores engulf London) and *Bedlam* (serial killer controls his victims' dreams), while *Carnosaur*, about genetically-recreated dinosaurs, preceded *Jurassic Park* by seven years.

R.A. Lafferty was a true original. Although he started writing seriously at an age when most people stop, he still did it better than most, and different to all. Following his debut in 1960, he produced more than 200 short stories and over twenty novels, including *Past Master, Fourth Mansions, The Devil is Dead* and *Serpent's Egg*. He won the 1973 Hugo Award for Best Short Story and the World Fantasy Award for Lifetime Achievement in 1990.

Samantha Lee re-wrote *Dr. Jekyll and Mr. Hyde* for a children's publisher and had to add a number of gruesome murders to delight the little terrors. More recently she has written a fantasy trilogy and a number of titles for Scholastic's young adult "Point Horror" series. However, she recently told us that she has given up writing horror for the moment, as there is already far too much of it in the real world.

Alan Moore has won every award it is possible for a comics writer to win. Having risen to fame with his scripts for DC Comics' *Swamp Thing* and the Hugo Award-winning *Watchmen*, in recent years his graphic series *From Hell, The League of Extraordinary Gentlemen* and *V for Vendetta* have all been filmed by Hollywood with varying degrees of success. Or not.

Kim Newman has won the Bram Stoker Award, the British Fantasy Award, the British Science Fiction Award, the Children of the Night Award and the International Horror Critics Guild Award. An author, reviewer and broadcaster, his many books include the acclaimed *Anno-Dracula* series, *Bad Dreams, Jago, Life's Lottery, Ghastly Beyond Belief* (with Neil) and *Horror: 100 Best Books* and *Horror: Another 100 Best Books* (both with Steve).

Ian Pemble trained as a chemist, but never practiced, instead he became a poet, an advertising copywriter and the editor of a naughty Men's magazine. These days he freely admits that he fantasizes less about sex and more about golf.

Terry Pratchett is the second most successful children's author in Britain. His phenomenally successful "Discworld" series has been published since 1983 and includes such titles as *The Colour of Magic, Mort, Wyrd Sisters, Guards! Guards!* and *Thud!*, along with all kinds of spin-off diaries, calendars, quiz books and collectible figures. He also co-wrote *Good Omens* with Neil, but that doesn't seem to have harmed his career.

Jessica Amanda Salmonson is the editor of the World Fantasy Award-winning anthology *Amazons!* and its sequel, plus *Tales by Moonlight* and the feminist collection *What Did Miss Darrington See?* Her other books include *A Silver Thread of Madness, Anthony Shriek, The Dark Tales* and *The Deep Museum: Ghost Stories of a Melancholic.*

Jody Scott is best known for her novels *Passing for Human* and *I, Vampire.* Her tendency in her fiction to take cockeyed ideas quite seriously is mitigated by her other tendency to treat things that most people take seriously – like Death and identity – with a sizeable pinch of salt.

S.P. Somtow was born in Bangkok, Thailand, and is the grand-nephew of the late Queen Indrasakdisachi of Siam. Renowned as a classical composer in his homeland under his real name, Somtow Sucharitkul, his books include *Vampire Junction, Moon Dance, The Pavilion of Frozen Women* and *Tagging the Moon: Fairy Tales from L.A.* He has also written and directed two feature films, *The Laughing Dead* and *Ill Met at Moonlight.*

Alex Stewart quickly discovered that his science fiction anthology *Arrows of Eros* was invariably referred to as "Sex in Space". He also devised the superhero anthology *Temps* with Neil. We're not sure if he still drinks Perrier without lemon.

David Sutton was recognized for his devotion to and achievement in the genre over many years with the British Fantasy Society's "Special Award" in 1994. He has also received the World Fantasy Award, The International Horror Guild Award and twelve British Fantasy Awards. He is the editor of a number of acclaimed anthologies, including *The Satyr's Head & Other Tales of Terror*, *Phantoms of Venice* and the *Dark Terrors* series (with Steve).

Gene Wolfe writes five pages each day, often rising at 5:00 or 5:30 A.M. to work before breakfast, and sometimes completing the fifth page around midnight. Every page of his stories receives at least three drafts and some go through ten or more. Despite this, he has written hundreds of short stories and dozens of novels, including the World Fantasy Award, Nebula Award and British Science Fiction Award-winning "The Long Sun" tetralogy.

ABOUT THE ARTISTS

Clive Barker is a one-man industry with books, movies, comics, art and toys based on his concepts. The author of the *Books of Blood* series, *Weaveworld*, *The Thief of Always*, *Coldheart Canyon* and the *Abarat* sequence (illustrated with hundreds of paintings by the author himself), he has directed the movies *Hellraiser*, *Nightbreed* and *Lord of Illusions*. When he didn't contribute a poem to this volume, we made him paint the frontispiece instead.

Andrew Smith used to draw cute fluffy animals for greeting card companies until he came to his senses. Since then, his distinctive monochrome and wash illustrations have graced a number of collections and anthologies, including several titles for the venerable Arkham House imprint. For this book, we asked him to draw some nasty fluffy animals . . .

Gahan Wilson believes he was helped to get off to a good start in the horror business by being born dead. He was saved only because the family doctor burst into the operating room and repeatedly plunged him first into a bowl of hot water and then into another filled with ice. Nowadays his work is mostly seen in *Playboy* and *The New Yorker*, while his macabre cartoons have been collected in a number of volumes, including *The Best of Gahan Wilson*.

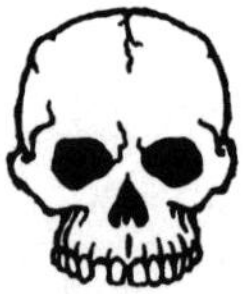